T0156619

SOUL *Thoughts*

Poetry for Our Growing Spirits

Celestial K.

iUniverse

SOUL THOUGHTS
POETRY FOR OUR GROWING SPIRITS

iUniverse books may be ordered through booksellers or by contacting:

iUniverse
1663 Liberty Drive
Bloomington, IN 47403
www.iuniverse.com
1-800-Authors (1-800-288-4677)

Because of the dynamic nature of the Internet, any web addresses or links contained in this book may have changed since publication and may no longer be valid. The views expressed in this work are solely those of the author and do not necessarily reflect the views of the publisher, and the publisher hereby disclaims any responsibility for them.

Any people depicted in stock imagery provided by Thinkstock are models, and such images are being used for illustrative purposes only.
Certain stock imagery © Thinkstock.

ISBN: 978-1-4917-5750-5 (sc)
ISBN: 978-1-4917-5751-2 (e)

Library of Congress Control Number: 2015900138

Printed in the United States of America.

iUniverse rev. date: 01/05/2015

Contents

SECTION I.   NATURE

SECTION II.   SPIRITUAL

SECTION III. LOVE

SECTION IV. FANTASY

SECTION V. MEMORIES

SECTION VI.   REMEMBERING MY GRANDFATHER

SECTION VII. CHANGE

SECTION 1

1   *Listening Souls*

Like a rope around
the rapidly beating hearts
of those feathered little creatures—
the birds—
is pulled by the sun,
they are awakened
by life breathing,
alight out of the meditation
of the night, and
begin to search for
listening souls
in chirping song.

2 Trapped in Beauty

Outside, the night-grass sings with
awakening insects.

Looking up, my mind wanders like it's in
a constant dream.

The stars hum with the vibration
of my subdued heart.

My true body belongs to sweet
nature.

My mind belongs to the
universe.

3 Canoe

The man walks down by the Arabia Mountain River Trail,
pushing his cedar-wood canoe.
The intense sweat feasts on his pores
as soon as he steps into the stifling Georgia heat,
but he continues like he enjoys it.
The scent of fresh leaves mixed with
the fluff of bird feathers are in the air.
The sharper branches whip his face as he makes
his way, but he acts like they are buddies holding
a friendly high-five.
He continues until his nose picks up the odor
of strong water. His face changes into brightness.
The glowing surface reflecting the sky,
but in a murky-greenish way, swirls in colors as if
a painter dipped his brush into a water cup
too many times.
Grunts, pushes the canoe into the water.
Ripples, out—out—out from the edge.
He steps inside, and pushes off.

4 *Pothos Plant*

Pothos:
simple. Easy to grow, but don't let that make you think
you're not something special.

Your traveling roots are lifeblood,
and as you rest and contemplate by the windowsill,
I faintly stroke you and breathe you in.

My dry fingers pack the dark, craggy soil around my plant,
lush sun-grown leaves stretching for me—
as I touch with my fingerprints' gentle caress,

a handshake between friends.
Limbs of vines, where will you grow next?
Twist around my skin and complete me.

Green as my first heart, like the Greek God
Pothos, longing, yearning to be loved, you
present your leaves to be kissed with soft human lips

so that you feel you are growing for something,
living for someone else, important life-form that you are.
Most fool their own hearts.

Water: because we can't all survive on just love,
the luscious sweet taste that you drain,
suck into yourself and shiver in contentedness.

I offer you the little care I can give, but I'll be watching how
you mature into a more capacious pot. I know you study
me as well, and try to understand how the stress

builds in my life, like in all humans. Don't try to fathom
our over-worked existence. Just be there for us.
Hold me in your exhalation of spirit.

Your colorful face is a daily lullaby to my eyes
and I am rocked to a soothing place in my soul
where I can be a simple smile.

5   *Clouded Light*

City that is always somber
with dark emotion of drooping rain
pauses.
I walk through thick shells of mist
and past the opaque, fattened
brick walls lacking moonlight
and it obscures my thinking—
until I find a slow-moving
inching
sun.

6 Splintered Bridge

The olden bridge is worn down—
the one that looms above the greenish
fishless pond.
It has veiny legs still standing
upright, somehow
holding.
Discoloration is splattered
amongst the wood
like a smudged photograph taken in
ancient years.
How many different kinds of
tree bark can combine
to keep this
pathway standing?
The splinters, once molded together,
start to separate slowly as they
drink in more rain.
The structure
aches.
Years prove it strong—
but still
do not trust
to cross over it.

7 *Moon Cave*

Darkness
pushes hard against the rock-strong cave
walls and dewdrop shaped roof,
as it stretches towards the
stone foundation like a melting candle.
Drippy sand.
Low oxygen.
The dank air stifles breaths,
but the brown bats
breathe just fine
in rapid-chest heaves through
a raspy throat.
They open and close green eyes
fast-blinking,
awaiting the moon but wishing
for light.

8   *Unconditional Love*

My pet lies anxiously,
brink of her fur perked, on edge,
waiting without moan
for me to finish my
important human business,
slow down
and to her,
speak.

9   *Lemon Plant*

She grows the lemon plant
in the hollowed clay pot
outside her front
door that swings wide only when friends
stop by—which is not often enough.

In secret, she pats
and fondles the moist dirt
and sings to the walking roots.
Soon she sees the ripening, yellow things
protrude

like miniature limp balls of
sour golden suns, which
with changing time of maturation,
grow harder,
flourish, and
remain unyielding to any destructive
elements of natural doom—

until she reaches out
her seeking hand
underneath the shading leaves,
her long fingers touching all around;

she finds one
and in a firm but soft grip,
pulls.
And then—the knife.

10 Seeing My Heart

Delicate animal,
her paws pressed on my shadow,
watches my every move—
her unblinking eyes,
dim with a milky
vortex,
tick greedily side to side:
like a lingering buzz
around my face,
pale hands, and hurried feet.

Even in her older age, as her movement
slows,
like an old priest who pauses to
think,
she can read me.
Unrevoked, still loving gaze
sees into me
as if the chest that holds my heart,
to her eyes,
is transparent.

11 Light from the Cedarwood Incense

Cedarwood burns slowly; the
smoke making pictures in the air
enters my lungs like a lullaby,
sweetly calming my mind.

The woody scent permeates my still being,
creates mind-drawn images of forests—
dozens of freshly grown trees,
married and thriving.
Me sitting
cross-legged on the dense dirt, pebbles, turning twigs
and comfortably focused. Sunrays skimming
through the stretching pines concentrate on arriving
to me and embracing.

My body strives for purity,
constantly checking itself.
Nothing I do seems good enough
and so I meditate on self-love.

I see the incense burning down slowly: the red, seared
light descending like an elevator to the bottom
of the hand-crafted clay holder, the ashes on the top
of the stick, not fallen down yet.

12 The Frog with Emerald Skin

Eyes blinking and bulging,
I see a gleam of heartfelt hope
emanating
as he glances at me—
the frog with emerald skin.

He oozes with the joy
of frolicking with his playmate Nature,
flipping and turning amongst
the flouncing wind and whirls of flying fallen leaves.

He: a tiny jewel of the meadow.
The Prince of the grass,
he knows.

Just like his, sometimes I wish
my home was outside and door-less,
my days following the sun—
fun-filled, unfettered and free.

I feel the warm pleasure
of all the forest creatures' gazes—
they watch my every move,
synchronize with my behavior.

My ungodly life stares
out from my mortal eyes, wishing
for more than we have:

no more wildlife drawn towards destruction,
species depleted,
hungry tongues to feed
unclean air—
it is all unneeded.

The frog with the emerald skin
gazes at me with a pure heart,
eyes of light, eyes of hope.

The window to a better world creaks open—
it is time to begin.

13 Where Beauty Rests

The sleepy rose of fragile figure
awakens from her twilight slumber
to find one of her soft petals
so flushed with pink color
but torn from some brush of
a hand
like a rip in a fine, silk dress
in which threads can't be fixed;
and she stifles a shocked sob,
but reasons that
at least her rose scent
has not diminished
in beauty.

14   Beneath the Waves

Beneath those waves of ocean that sputter
blue-frilled foam and spit at me pieces of a
hello—

below that false-faced blank reflection
of the ever-watching, gently waiting
moon—

silently swim, grow and collect
bubbling, flipping
life forms,

completely unknown,
and not at all
understood.

15 Innocuous Existence

The sun lays itself down to rest
in the orange color of rooted emotion and
a lengthy span of cardinal red, both wordlessly
spread over the calm pasture of gray,
peeking headstones.

So many names
alive now only in calligraphy.
So many scripts
captured with words of goodbye.

Yet deep below, the deceased are
still somewhere alive and celebrating
transitions that are brighter than
death first appeared.

Perchance, they are inside the Earth
stretching their tense muscles long for
an extensive finale dance. The coffin is an illusion
and the path to the innocuous existence.

I sweep my feet away,
and towards the graveyard gates the
blinking sun falls to sleep,
and in the distance, new colors peep—
butterflies rise.

16 Shiver

Meow!
Her hairs stand up
white as a frightened ghost,
but no one is there to hear her
cry out.

17 Sky Panegyric

Today on the balcony
I saw the summer sun
become a ballerina, slowly bending
down in complete balance to touch
her toes.
I thought of you
until the sky filled my heart instead.

The shifting firmament of awe
was more agape than usual—
like a ravenous mouth
sweating with desire—
or giant, arms stretching beyond boundaries,
yet missing something
at the same time,
like anticipating a hug
that won't approach.

I realized
I can't compete with the celestial sky.
I am nothing.
Insignificantly existing.

The dark clouds peppered
the air with accented polka dots, and
others were graying deep,
elongated like an old man's
twisted beard.

The sky was so steady and still,
all heard me inhale.
Paint-less painting,
this immortal being was a slowly
fading picture, ever modifying;
but my eyes missed it
if they moved just a fracture.

The hidden horizon-clouds slept low,
highlighted around the edges
like an otherworldly glow.

With full eyes, my gaze snaked
beyond the tips of those composed trees,
and then my mind saw it.
Within the clouds:
a wide-floored city
with tiny building roofs
popping up.
A Kingdom so close I could see myself
living inside
as if it was my Utopian home
with all the blessed others that made it to
this special realm.

Slamming desire
to break my body and fly
my soul towards the city of
Olympia—
Heaven—
the great Nirvana—
overcame me.

Eyes mesmerized.
Was it in truth
just whitened mist
in the air? Clouds symbolize
God's dream for us.
Fingers reaching.

Eye-moisture welled with heart-longing.
Afraid to leave—for everything would change
into a disappeared sight so quickly.

The Fairy-lit trees became enchanted shadows,
fading away from the sun into themselves;
but my paradise vision glowed.
The gods beckoned me.

I couldn't hear the crunching sound of
rolling skateboards on black cement
by unconcerned teenagers underneath me.

I couldn't focus on the woman rushing
out of the apartments for her car,
shoe-heels clacking towards me.

I ignored the blinking lights of the
flight abounded airplanes trying to ruin
my sight's bliss.

It called me too strongly.
Hands on the wooden balcony railings,
then feet on the edge,
I stood,
and flew.

18 Rainbow Release

I see it—
a rainbow—colors like
a new, wild Earth
just forming and
sprouting fresh ideas of
Life.

It is a symphony
of growth surrounded by
warmth after heavy storms.

Yet fresh raindrops gather
within the distant clouds like a
mother gathers her children,
to protect them
only till a certain time—
the right time,
to release.

19 Revive from Darkness

The work-clock drains me.
Part of my mind is dead daily at this time—
the piece that contains my soul.
Many hours pass until I am
freed.

The night has birthed us another
fulgent moon so we don't roam in
complete fear and cognizant
darkness.

Outside on my porch, the savory air smells of
(sadly) distant oaks and sunsets gone,
of blood that was drawn from roses and faded
into some kind of berry-sweetness.

My heart beats like a weak lamb's coo.
The cool wind enjoys the feel of my skin, wants
to take its breath away. Goosebumps jump high.
I am cradled in the grasp of my own mortal thoughts.

Our lives are often performed within
walls closed to nature's reality.
My kidnapped energy must be
revived by vital nature.

Between the edges of my terminal life,
I thought I was weak.
But buried strength learned to ascend
like forest smoke.
I keep surviving. I am
mighty.

20 Outside of the Hypnotic World

The squeaking screen door bounces once
in a frolic behind me
and snaps shut.

Instantly the sun lurches
lithe, affable arms in my direction.
In this moment, that warm star

is as close to me as the
worm-chewed dirt beneath my
freed toes.

My smile remembers it has
effulgent rays of its own
and emerges.

The promiscuous pine needles
play catch with my hair,
tossing my fragrance.

I succumb to the muggy
weather, the
raindrop-permeated air.

Lock the door from the
inside,
and never let me reenter

the hypnotic world
of false, mind-bending comforts
that never satiate.

Where Earth, air, flame, and water
meet—this is where I'm meant to be—
my first home.

21 Ballet of the Storm

Before a storm comes,
nature jitters with excitement—
dogwood trees sway their midsections,

and their branches extend like skeletal fingers,
shuddering as wind laughs, springs up,
and pirouettes through their rustling limbs.

Newly departed leaves scatter—
crunch across the shadowed asphalt
and gleefully slide into people's yards.

The gray-hazed sky rumbles with
elated commotion
as it watches the ballet underneath.

The sun decides to embrace secrecy, eclipsed;
the rain begins a cooling, gentle cascade.
But, the humans close their doors.

SECTION 2

Spiritual

22 Pure Spirit

The stars
gasp as the milk
of the universe sprays
infinitely and shines on them
like God.

23 The Light in the Painting

And they pose to be remembered.
Look deeper into the portraits
of the past—can their sacred-held souls still
shine through? The painting by a
man of the ultimate mother and
child, baby of God, is too valuable
to touch by tainted human hands.
Too holy for fingerprints. It is such a
kind scene. Instead, your eyes can
gently explore the painted marks
and pretend this display is real.

Gaze into the mother's eyes
filled with weariness of the previous
adventure, preparing yet for much
more. She wraps the small blanket
around a shivering child, but she can
still sense, if she closed her eyes, the
warm glowing aura, lustrous and beaming
from her newborn's head—and she
has hope for the divine day that will
come when that light would extend itself
to all the world—all the nations that
deserve this special blessing of peace.

Soft expressions are seen upon
her face and are felt within her cheeks
when she smiles and looks down.
The infant's fist, meek upon her breast,
produces yet no wrinkle upon her
faded clothes. The perfect hand
is kissed by her lips, claiming him
for now. But He soon will be shared.
The Mother's eyes meet the artist.
She and her Son become still,
and they pose to be painted.

24 *Holding Onto an Angel*

My Angel watches me, my every motion,
and knows she moves so differently.

It is effortless to float between dimensions;
but Angels can't feel life like this.

She doesn't know what it's like
to breathe in air that the lungs crave,

to pulse those blood-beats from her
neck, wrist-veins and chest,

to faint from ocean-heavy tears
and succumb to her fortified fears,

to feel too full from a bloating meal
or mad starvation in the saddest sense.

She can't admire through unique human eyes
the violet-filled flowers

bloomed and flushed, that I glance at
on my rushed march from my apartment

to my injured car, heading again towards
my confidence-discarding workplace.

She has no heart which can be filled
or pour out strong sensations of love

or broken into pieces.
She doesn't have the understanding

of the pressures of mortality, the
terror of painful, plodding death, or of

constant fights with the snarling beasts
that dwell in the devil-corners of the mind.

She cannot become attached to me
as a mother, as a friend, or as a lover.

She loves me, but she doesn't know why.
My Angel touches me, and wonders.

25 Spirit of Illusions

I'm pouring out my spirit.
Let it parade alone
on all the grassy plains
and frigid mountain ranges of Earth,
where it can't really feel
or breathe, but just
exist in unattached observation.

I seek no answers despite
my eyes of grim confusion.

I grasp hold of once-important things
that aren't real anymore; deniable.
It seems as if everything is
a glassy, bright-eyed illusion
that slips through the broken fingers
of the gasping ghosts that have stayed here,
like a façade covering crumpling flowers.

26 Upwards, the Sky

Passion suffused gazes
climb upward
alight—

heavens ablaze like an inferno
in the mind center of the sky.
All eyes see and feel

the Earth: pulses,
agitated shakes,
vomit of pinching poison

multiplied
amongst us.
We raise our hands

and our souls signal to the misty
atmosphere for help.
Reach further.

Inside us deep
the mass of Angel voices
whispers

to believe in the goodness
that is lost
within ourselves.

27 The Master Spoke

The people gathered.
The dust coughed at my feet
like the sun caught a cold.
I empathized with the clouds,
their cheeks too red.
I raised my arms in a blessing.
The people gathered and
listened.
Stillness became the event.
Even the dust settled
and sat attentively.
God's words are
my power.
I breathed in
and spoke of love.

28 Inside Stillness

Eyelids flutter
furiously—not wanting to look inside.
It has been so long since they
took a look at my heart;
they are embarrassed.

Shaking hands, upturned lips—
always a proper greeting that
shows that all is welcome here.
Slowly opening my chakra like waking petals—
de-cluttering the mind.

Flowing gray beats and red beats—
sometimes I read the beats
of the pumping organ that lets me know
I am alive.
But what does that signify?

Hands can hold, grasp other fingers
and have a candied feel;
and watches can tick and stick to my wrist
as sea waves breathe their death on
the shore that I grew up on.

Eyes, listen closely;
my soul doesn't speak.

29 Gods in the Air

The gods
with a smile blithe
chew, tear, munch on
fried clouds—
such a delicacy.

30 The Peeking Soul

I'm coming apart,
shedding like a snake undressing silvery skin:
sliding off and crumbling down.
When the slithering thing moves away,
his body is fresh, anew.

This outer me peels and falls away fiercely
like weighty rocks declining from a mountain—
wheeling aside, crashing downward as
the waters below devour them
and digest each slab whole.

Once all my flesh is taken
by the greedy gravity of Earth,
I will be gone, but complete.
All that will be left to view
is not my broken heart or skulled head, but soul.

31 Teenager Jesus and Wine

Dear Mother of my heart,
before your complaints, I'll say my part.

Your lined face is haggard, stressed,
your shoes worn down, your hair a mess.

But I know something that will make it all fine,
you see, I can turn pure water into wine.

I don't know what happened to me,
I just touched the water, imagining.

What escaped was a silly, trifling thought
and I hoped and prayed I wouldn't get caught.

But I see you found where I hid the stash;
I know you're angry, but don't be rash.

God gave me this gift; I know not why,
and now all my friends want to give it a try.

Here, taste the liquid that was dipped in berries
growing in a spellbound garden with the juiciest cherries.

Doesn't it taste quite luscious and sweet?
Now every day, our meals can be a feast!

Each Passover and Seder I'll bless us with home-made wine
that will cost us nothing but my concentration time.

I've been making barrels of it every day, for free!—
no I offer many others to drink some, not just me.

Don't worry, I sturdily hold onto sobriety
by consuming only two goblets a day, maybe three.

Drink some more, Mother, of my impressive heavenly gift!
I can create more than sturdy muscles can lift.

I'm now the most popular, sought-out guy in class;
after showing my magic, I was popular fast.

To all the cool parties, I'm given an invitation
and when I alter their water to wine, it's a celebration.
What? They only like me for my "magic trick?"
Well then, I won't heal them if they get sick.

But, I'm Jesus—I'm too enlightened to be malicious.
I'll keep it all for us, then—the wine, red or white—delicious!

You're always right, Mother, this wine-making is a fad…
I hope my punishment isn't so horribly bad.

32 Lotus Pose

My body crossed in Lotus Pose,
my heart feeling limber and light,
palms resting up in a waiting charade,
ready for sweet changes to come to me—
like the optimism in the savory scent that coffee
gives each waking person in the darkness
of the mornings without daylight shining yet.

If I stay still in Lotus Pose—
neglect the boorish-mouthed television news
that revels in marring my soul like
all those heart-wrenching murders they
show, ignore the pain of our existence
because there's nothing I can do about it—
I might just feel hope for the world.

33 Aged Planets

Planets sometimes resting,
sometimes running in a spiral
track across the widened galaxy,
high-five each other as they pass.

It is not a race, they know,
because when they get to
the end, it is
a bitter end.

Still, their outer skin grays
eventually, and they age to be
great-great-great grandparents,
wise in all the years of
teaching and astute learning.

A sensible thing: for us to listen to them.
God created them to
live so much longer
than us.

This must mean that
He truly trusts them.

34 The Angel Walks Among Us

The Angel walks among us
with feet not from this world…

down those crowded school halls where
that five-year-old child got shot dead
and ten are injured…

in that promised-gloom side street
where the frantic woman begged for life,
then threw her purse to
run the other way…

into the ocean as the sunken passengers
cling to each other and their
mind-frozen memories…

into the deserts of distant disease and
wretched starvation, fastening
hands to stomach like food…

The Angel sees and knows,
but can't cherish life like we do.

Isolated beauty,
you catch my muttered prayers.

Thank you—
The Angel sees me.

35 Walk of Milk and Honey

Patience is
frustration cleverly covered
under wrinkled skin
while following Moses
in the deserts
for forty years.

36 The Pen Mark

God's pen
is named Divine
and shines ink that is star-golden.

I ask Him to look over
my current book of Life
and to add whatever He thinks
should come next.

I am welded to the flesh
and have endured continued wrecks;
but, whichever way He marks,
my spirit will discover the way.

My own stammering pen has faltered,
printing mistakes in my story, and now they will
be patched. My soft-soul Angel is here
beside my straying shoulder.

I half-smile because I know
the future will begin things
and not end them. Our lives
can always be birthed again.

Hold my hand, and I will
show the Devil not fear
but love, because
I can.

God nods, understands,
and His Divine pen
marks a page.

SECTION 3

Love

37 Soul Heart

Even though it's short,
in the irreplaceable time
we are connected,
skin-shell boundary-less,
flawless,
broken edges meshed,
breaths together in
and out,
our minds trust
and believe
for the first time
that we are just
two perfect souls
swimming
in one.

38 A Parting Kiss

Midnight, he sits on the silvered bolder
away from the rushed world.

Upright stone pieces pinch his backside;
he shifts in his dark blue beltless jeans, and wraps his
thin jacket around him tighter against a coming
wind. He hopes she is warm tonight.

Placing two joined fingers together upon his upturned lips,
he parts a soft kiss.

Hand out to the wind, he lets it lift his hair,
small particles of dust and skin, and his blown kiss.
He watches it ascend into the shaded clouds as
they abound and embrace each other,
bringing in the certain heart-turning tempest.

As the drops begin to fall, splitting into a thousand
wet pieces upon his uncovered head, he openly receives the
cooling calm—a gift of Angels, a peace settling
his heart.

His kiss has reached her
in his mind.

The storm begins.

39   The Rose Flaunts

The flower flaunts its body,
draping over
the side of the outdoor table.

Heart-stopping red with curls
inside that spiral into
another world that I can't see.

There's more to this piece of Earth
than what meets the human eye.
You stole it from Heaven,

I'm sure.
Its sweet smell drifts like
the hope inside a beautiful sunset

and sails outward.
Everyone on the street stops
to stare—their boring walk made

beautiful.
My lucky heart sings,
because you are just here.

This is our first
date, and our last
search for love.

40 *Heart Fireworks*

I can feel the sparks shoot from the
crackling charcoal under the grill,
watch the Georgia sunset intensify to the indigo color that
I remember from once long ago, and I feel like
I'm back in a childhood memory.

But the difference is now I'm with you,
holding on to the dreams that we will effortlessly create
our own family one day—with little ones running around,
wind braiding their hair and smeared dirt marks
on their sun-reddened cheeks of happiness.

The firecrackers start booming, crashing into streams
of colors high up beyond the tree branches as we watch
and hold hands on the soft blanket sheltering the grass.
Fireworks of love and hope roar, too, in our hearts,
displayed in twisting rainbows across the widened sky.

41   Our Room

I will empty out your heart
and then place all my possessions
within it. Object after object,
the room will become warmer,
consuming the air like a cozy
fire in the corner. Pictures of my
childhood paintings will be hung
on the walls, your floor carpeted
with all my dreams of our future.
Music of love that I composed just
for you shall flow from room to
room, and I will turn up the volume
until it reaches all ears. I then will
bake sugared cookies to welcome myself
into your heart, and the sweet smell
of them shall invade the air, and stick
itself to all the sweaters and pillowcases
and bed sheets that once were
yours but now are my own. I shall see into
the deepest part of your soul and walk
along the shore until I see your past loves
that hardened into shells. Those rotting sea-shells
of old and ancient passions that still cling
to you as if you were theirs—you have left
them scattered around your random ocean.
You thought all this was lost to my eyes, but
I see—I am throwing these shards away.
Say *goodbye.*

Your shore will be bare, and I shall place
my footprint upon the sand, feel secure, and
then return to the room which is mine.
I will become the guardian of the door to
your heart, standing strong. The people who
dare to attempt to enter shall die before they
cross the threshold. No one else allowed in.
Don't worry, my dear, I shall speak for you;
I shall speak through you when they question us.
I shall hold you in my arms, wherever you are,
and whisper to you, as I am inside of you,
and you become me.

42 Speak to Me

Your breath is my slippery siren,
luring me to uneven waters
where the unknown and fear can be deep-felt,
if not still misunderstood.

Your departing words are my eternity
as soothing rain tapping my freckled skin
gasping out, and melting, sinking in:
speak to me, speak again.

Your voice plays tag in my nerves, and
tugs all that I am—entangles me,
the sole world of allurement,
where I am happy, enthralled to be tied
to you.

43 Something Waits

In the future's distanced sight
I see what is to come.

Your eyes will still look at me like this
in twenty years, because

I make it so; as if everything is
new—an unexpected present on

an unanticipated, gleeful day. Waiting reminds
me of those two red wine bottles,

sealed since my birthday, you bought and
told me to save for a special day.

Those cherry phenomenons are like posed gymnasts
in a skilled handstand on the coiled wine rack,

still and waiting, barely breathing,
knowing that one day I will come and

rescue those clutched breaths. Dust is flicked off
occasionally as I do my cleaning rounds.

The wine waits, but the years don't halt
and time grins as it waves goodbye.

44 Teddy Bear with the Button Eyes

He looks like a Teddy Bear.
A stuffed animal awaiting my arms,
here for me to grab tight and
squeeze to my chest with all
assurance that he will not die.

Funny how over time, he has become
deformed. His eyes look more like
buttons, and his hands are non-responsive
paws. Pleading him to hold my hand.
For him to want to cleave to me is getting
harder. He no longer reacts to my tears.

I can move his spiritless arms and fists where
he lacks the strength of will to. I can make
him clench my palm, force him to pretend
to love me fleetingly. On the outside, he is a bear.
On the inside, he is cloudy stuffing.

What scares me is that I cannot stay
away from this teddy of mine. Over time,
my thoughts and emotions will be replaced
by cotton. People will question where my
soul is. My eyes will become
buttons like his.

45 Blue Jay

When the running water
cuts my beaten skin
from hot to
cold
like a dagger to
fresh red meat,
my lonely blood
knows
you are gone
away
just like
the rejected blue jay
that appears traveling
in spurned flight,
shivering and sodden-looking
in the falling snowflake's
slim reflection…
smaller and
soon digested completely
in the frozen heart
of the winter sky—
as if it never
existed.

46 *Bouquets of Death*

He sends me the flowers,
blooming and blushing and
pink. Just for me, to cheer me
up. I pretend that he gave
them to me with a kiss of love;
but he sealed it with a
little card, handwriting not
trying for beauty. He signed
it with his name—not quite
a kiss.

Now upon my desk for all to
see—all who enter my room.
Not many do. But they are
there anyway. The blossoms
with the coral bow. They sit
and they wait. The nights send
them to sleep. They are slowly
deformed with time. I still keep
them here: withered, crisp and dark.
Even when dead, they are sweet.

47 Eternal Embrace

Here, in the abysmal-consumed waves, steal me
away from me. I feel strange comfort in your silent,

lascivious eyes, wanting me, yet not knowing how—
but I whisper: *Just take me.*

We hold our burden of breaths as we watch
the aged ocean suck itself back in,

scraping the sharp, coiled seashells
and wailing with the lustful wind.

The world doesn't need us.
I lean in to hear your murmur of hushed tones.

Only here is where we belong, forever on the shore.
Your embrace has become my world.

48 My Soul Breathes

My soul moves, it breathes.
Inside me it lives and sings.
With paints that drip off the galaxy-stars,
my soul is an artist. With sunken space
as her art canvas, she makes a mural with
all the colors that are her favorite.

They swirl, they shine, they glow
and come alive, creeping up from the paper,
inching towards bright, peeking eyes.

Deep, meditative wisdom knows
this special design was made for the soul-mate
who will match his colors with mine.

The colors can blend together
in paintings' creative kiss,
as our hearts blur in spirit-embrace.
Who has eyes to see through dimensions
and can spot the vision of the future
artwork of our existence together?

Most people view me as a passing stranger:
a fleeting, insignificant part
in the whole that is his life, but
someone someday will know…
will see my color-coated picture and my waiting being,
look in my eyes and understand all.

He will promise a kiss in his eyes
that shakes my heart-core—
my soul breathes—
that is my soul—
the caress becomes me.

49 Home of Illusion

My hazy dream
plays on.

A home of hearts, with
laughter decorating every room,
but my prettiest piece of
furniture is you.

Lounging in a bed of stars
after cooking a succulent dinner,
the unwinding melodies swaying
our minds to sleep.

I feel warmth seeping from our febrile
skins. You've wrapped your soul
around my wrists, and I give in to you
as my castle of man.

My dream of peace
plays on, and even if
it's never real,
my heart feasts.

50 The Midnight Bridge of Stars

Midnight, walking on the bridge. The one
in the city, but you can barely see the buildings

unless you stand at a certain point.
They transformed into shadows with ghost-lit windows.

We stopped and gazed off into the dark horizon,
and stopped again to feel each other's arms.

Our glances faced directly ahead at the oncoming
car lights that I wished would stop so we could be

completely alone. Eyes not seeing as
much as skin does. Our souls felt each other out.

My senses became your arms
covering me like a tender army of protection

against the oncoming moonlit air, which made everything
colder, fainter, thinner—except our growing hearts.

My curious eyes glanced at you, peeling your clothes
off like loosened flesh with my gaze,

but then all I could do was lose balance in the blueness of your
ocean-eyes, moving pools of joy and gladness that you found me.

51 Soul Absorption

Your dreams and hopes collect in your
voice of thickened sugar
exuding steadiness for me—you
are suddenly everywhere.
Sound is nothing until
it touches the walls of my body
and is slowly drunk,
sucked inwards
gently until
my soul feeds
on your words.

52 Ghost Kiss

Gentle wind moves through me
like I'm just another willow tree, standing.

I strain my fingers, spread wide
reaching for some part of you.

My nails catch—I pull you in,
even though you're invisible,
and I kiss your ghost.

Sweet taste
I relish.

Why, my heart…
my imagination!

53 Shining Eyes, Glowing Breaths

I want to breathe out
and know you're there in the space close by,
exhaling with me.

Feel your hand so present,
centered with ease, swimming in
the river of my aura;
I can take it in mine.

I'm selfish and full of desperate greed
because I need more than one
half-spent lifetime with you. More than two.
My prayers plead—anything to keep you forever.

Your sea-filled eyes are beautiful pools of
blue star-suns open to all the Earth.
Black space splashes inside you,
your bloodline of stars intense, but invisible.

I must claim your universe
as mine.

54 Of Time

Jealous of Time because
it keeps you in a callous, strange grasp,
and yet you, on your bruised knees,
worship it
and I cannot compare
to deserve that praise.
Time: so expansive and never-ending.
Consistently deadly.

Short times we were together
do not begin to amount
to all the dreadful time apart,
mounting slowly to a horror of the years;
and no matter how I scream or
giggle or blush or profusely bleed,
I cannot break free from the loneliness
Time gave me.

Time is the meeting place
of relationships, and yet it sneaks
masked as if it's the greatest murder
weapon for the death of love.
It keeps us in a place—
whenever it wants—
although our own desires
are crushed helpless.

I guess
you were never mine.
We all belong to Time.

55 Hold Tightly

Her breaths are like the ocean,
foaming and moaning and
coming up and then back down
on soft spread sand dimly reflecting a
darkened-night moon glow.

Arms wrapped tight, like the white
strings of a kite gone dancing around
the wrist of a child, suffocating till the blood
pushed back.

Her sweet scent always draws your
soul like universe's fate—inescapable,
the past so there and the
future so faint.

If you let her go,
the night will terminate itself,
and all the goodness of life
will flicker, fall, fade.

56 Through My Heart's Dancing Eyes

Delicate skin clings to Angel-soft bones
as we possess each other's hands on the color-changing
beach of our holiday—sky from apricot to freshly squeezed
orange pulp and then to a steady pink like blushing sunbeams.

My heart is an eternal merry-go-round at nightfall.
The molded horses of paint and colors dance up and
down without moving their legs, gently swaying to a tinkling
tune of lip-blown flutes and deep, grave whistles,

sounding as a child's first music box
that you play over and over as he falls
asleep again, again—his drowsy eyes starting to
concentrate sleepily on a dream.

SECTION 4

Fantasy

57 Dragon Mounting and Departure

I rode a dragon barefoot.
Bet myself I couldn't—and go!
Jumped on his back, arms spread wide,
landed and grabbed with sweaty palms and stretching toes
onto the slippery scales that glistened
the rainbow colors like jewels and gold—
mesmerized my eyes—
I couldn't wait to fly!

So tower-tall was he. Burning breath released, scalding as
the blue center of a deadly flame. Stars melted as he tried
to get me—tail like a gigantic snake
swishing slowly back and forth—
but such muscles!
Heart pulsating, his wings began to beat—
like helicopters belaboring in my ears—
then, we were off!

58 The Sound of Hope

Fairy
wings tinkling
like a choir of peace
in my ready ear, listening
for change.

59 Poltergeist Sings

Years-splattered
piano bench creaks
as he sits—the fearful black keys cry,
weep, then succumb
to the ghost touch.
Dismal drops of music in minor
sputter into the dusty air—
gray clouds of sinister feelings—
and seep into the pausing
souls of the walls—
a wailing that only
loss is familiar with.
He yearns for life
or someone else's death.
Don't listen.
The poltergeist sings.

60   Wishes and Waltzes

If my wishes were put together,
counted and collected and
specifically selected,
I would, with the magic of my heart,
transform them into Time—

Time I take that gives me
space to breathe and think and
rest with head submerged in pillows of comfort
deep, completely mine, with no worries
of future or past, just that the

here and now would last and last
until I took a blade and decisively
killed the horrid enemy Time.
Finally.
My best lover would be my freedom

and in our waltzes birth a kingdom
of everlasting peace.

61 Games with Cat and Fairy

With graceful legs and a daring
swish of her cat tail,
she crouches down like under a wicked hunt,
where she can win the big prize
or die a solid fight.

With an aura so gentle,
the Fairy floats, flits, flies above her head,
acute cat ears pointed, flexing, flicking,
twitching to hear it right.

Enchanted laughter in her ears,
the cat growls and frolics her eyes around,
follows the every move of the winged
being, knowing magic light follows it
instead of a shadow.

Pouncing with a clawless move of grace,
the cat attacks and the Fairy laughs.
She can't catch her, but it's a fun game;
living and loving, their hearts are filled the same.

62 *Fear Not the Window*

Don't fear them when they come for you
in the sky-dead night, the waning moon
just watching it all happen—egging them on.

Their ship that has traveled space—
breathed among the stars—parked
in quiet outside your parent's house.

They come seen, then unseen,
through your window—closed or open.
They find a way to take you.

But don't fear them when they come for you
because that will make them stronger.
Instead, look at them—

see them for who they truly are—
aliens not any better, not much different,
than how you were made.

You will not be hurt—
trust in something in your heart.
Small smile, then pray.

63 Belonging

I belong to a place
just as lovely as this,
but one supplying people
evolved in the essence of
compassion. Kind words spill plentiful,
and honeyed laughter begins
each luminous day.
Moments are reveled in,
never wasted, and
regrets and mournful wishes
never surface to the lips.

I belong to a place,
where the people and land are one
with each other, and each heart beats
together, goals synthesized—
where love is godly
and shared just as purely.
Upon the warm breezes,
melodic music reaches and hugs the soul
and lifts the heart up high.
One can never be too happy there,
and no one is anything but.

I belong to a place
as beautiful as this,
except all the land there
was left undestroyed
and thrives in vibrant blessing.
I miss the kindness,
I crave the deep companionship,
I long for the healing land and people.
All my love is left there
flourishing where I am not;
and I cannot return.

64 Soul Dance of Hope

My soul sways with the beat of the Fairies,
in the hope that cares are far away,
and that all that matters is what happens today,
here and now upon the mobile planet:

and me and my feet and how they balance on air
and how my hair breaks the exhaled wind
and my smile attempts permanence—everlasting,
just like in the face of my Fairy-friend—

our unfaltering grins like our bond—enduring.
I can't help but feel my spirit ripple,
first in small bubbles, then in a happy rupture,
as my aura shines with pure perfection
and I multiply my hearts' affection.

I am as positive as the swirled stars
that I gaze upon in my dizzying spin;
I feel an unseen power, like I can donate happiness
to the people of the world.

I just hope some people can feel
the little sprites flitting by their ear
and know above all that someone is there,
arms surrounding, watching over them.

65 The Porcelain Clan

As a vampire,
I stand with my

clan, still and unmoving—porcelain
as the cold, hushed heart within.

Starving eyes redden and wait to
feed on the fleeting coats of

forest-dwelling animals.
But my favorite bloodbath—

teeth immersed in sweet wrist-veins,
done all to view my collection

of high-school graduation
caps: my success in life.

66 Unexpected Aid

This pink-flushing Fairy trails in the dense woods
turning bright with the falling sunbeams.

Crickets vocalize softly at first,
as the moon sticks her chest out

proudly. She has entered the scene.
Shadows gently chew on the leaves

until even branches are consumed,
and the daylight is only alive in the

areas where humans keep their constant
lights blazing too brightly to see the

stars. The Fairy raises her arms to the
night and welcomes sleeping life.

Crouched in the hollow of the gaping pine,
she waits until the others start their dance.

Magic thrown off their wings, they gradually,
gradually heal the sickened Earth.

67 Failed World

I tried to create
a new world—with waters resplendent beautiful,
sublime oxygen of happiness, and
sacred grounds of overflowing peace.

The plans of bliss were set,
and it was made, paradise brave;
and I welcomed all the sad souls from this world,
told them they can be happy again.

They tried to live there, and for
a little while, all was pleasant perfection.
But soon they could not endure it.
Pacing, I couldn't understand it.

Heart-excitement was missing,
body aching thrills, and mind throbbing horror—
none were found. No traces of
dirty deaths and sinking sorrow.

The world was a bought brand of Heaven,
ideal everything, chiseled perfection in each
bone-made structure, but *it lacked life*,
the people said.

One by one, they left my world
to live upon the old Earth on their own.
And soon enough, I joined them
so I wasn't alone.

68 Stardust Tears

When your eyes cry, stardust
puffs and spreads outwards
like a sore gift from the heavens
exiting from your holy tear ducts,
and the dust of the stars
cascades slowly down your
pearl-soft cheek, and silently spills
to the wetted ground like a glassy
rainfall;
the drops quench the
dark soils' thirst and it drinks them in,
in,
in,
until there is nothing left
to satisfy.
Our Earth becomes impregnated from
your stardust tears,
and infant bodies sprout
in weak trees, shrubs, flowers, and leaves,
until they all age,
grow strong,
and tilt their faces upward,
looking back
to the heavens.

69　Anguta the Ferryman

Adlivun:
the world that shimmers just underneath the surface
of the dimension of the living.

Called the underworld, and yet
it is only dark when the people sleep
with their spirit-eyes closed and
move like slow-motion in their breathless dreams.

Otherwise, light sneaks and reflects off
of the steady, unmoving sea,
from the unnoticed stars that
shine faintly above a murky death-sky;
and yet, the waters alone
rest in a constant stare at them.

Anguta's paddle of gold dips in
the pool of stillness,
guided by the black otters
and underwater whales who do not surface to see him.
They are too big, and
their lungs no longer need the movement of breath.

The dead people stare at him as
they sit in his boat, hearing the ripples
scarcely splashing the sides of the vessel
like a pacifying lullaby.

This is not your slumber yet, he says.
I am taking you to sleep. Dream for a year.
Dream and forget. You don't need to feel
anything anymore.

70 Good Magic

I'll draw you a dragon
if you paint me a princess.

Destructive and violent—
she is better than my best.

I want a pleasant picture
to place on the wall: of a

pink girl with shining gem-eyes,
a dress of heavy gold, and

her fingers scintillating
with underlying magic—

a lost land to my era,
playtime fantasy and yet real.

I fall hypnotized into this image.
They will wonder where I am.

The welcome portal opens up
and ingests me alive

as my skin becomes acrylic,
and my eyes cry no more.

Forever a painted smile imbedded on me,
as I hold the prince's arm.

Forever I doze inside my home—
the castle that protects my life.

Forever I'll live in my universe,
happily ever after.

71   Magic of the Broom

Riding on a broomstick must be done
with a different one than you actually sweep with—
pick one with good-scented wood,
strong beneath your tingling finger's grasp.

You might feel the steady handle flutter,
joy-quiver under your magic palm—
excitement spreading inside its spine.
It's always gratified to be your ride.

It will *whish* and *whoosh* under your feet,
your new dancing-partner, and ballerina leap
in a swinging motion down your
waxed and chase wooden floor.

And then, wait for the fullest moon,
white as ghostly-turned candlelight,
watching and guiding the witch-ridden flight.
Only then, like your heart, can the broom rise.

72 Ring Around the Rose

Blood-red rose withered,
bends its heavy-hearted head,
petals curled and forlorn.
It is empty-alone,
like the galaxy moved over a step
to give her a space all to herself,
unwanted.

Until the translucent wings bat
and the little feet push off from the ground,
putting the Fairies of hope into flight.
They dance around the depressed beauty-flower
and in spurts of magic sparks are born;
faster they fly, faster around in their
Fairy circle.

The tiniest bubbles of spurted light
begin to swirl around her,
like a ripple in a broken water,
growing in fascinated delight.
Rose opens her heavy arm-petals
touches the sun, then
feels her lifted, beating heart.

SECTION 5

73 Time for Wine

Wearied head, heavy from the day, is
blurred with conversations pivoting through
me.

I see blue reflections on the fine, clear glass,
curved and ready for my lips.
It almost shimmies with excitement.

Open cabinet door, I stretch upwards, dancing on my tiptoes
like I was a formal ballerina, and how I wish
I had that grace.

Reaching, touching past the wooden shelf,
my fingerprints now painted
on the elegant cup—marked as mine.

The berry-red wine gurgles through the pointed
aerator. The glass half-full of precious promises.
Come to me.

You are mine tonight.

I anticipate the bell—
the hollow ghost-moan of ages
like a wandering spirits' reverberating shout
continuing from 1858.

Big Ben halts from his thoughts,
determined stance guarding the silvery-swirled
waters, reflecting a goldness the
rare sun-face mirrors.

No one's vision was grayed today by
gloom-spreading plumped raindrops
that usually ached to travel: to zip down
people's heads or slide off their black,

sleek, prepared umbrellas proper,
as if the little wet things
were tiny beasts of harm, full snarl,
growling by day and night.

Not now. I peer at the steady
boat-collecting water, watching
the glows and sparkles of surreal sunrays—
I am here to listen to your bell chime—

winded, air-warping sound,
soul-cutting,
skin-jumping,
bells.

75 Blue Thoughts

The pool water she thrived in
was small and dirty.

The one she should have lived in
was a blue abyss; an ocean far and deep—

a universe whose wide arms
reach and stretch to where the end

becomes the beginning, but
you can never get there.

Still, the water cradled us, and the
gray Dolphin was a friend.

I took hold of her fin like it was
an offered hand, and we took a stroll.

She wanted to tell me something,
a message on the tip of her beak.

Some secret she knew about life,
about touching happiness and keeping it.

But once our dance was over, a picture was
snapped brightly, and she swam away.

76   Day Memories

On some nights I find that I have time
to look up and gaze at the ceiling—
speckled with the rough convex plaster
pumping through the white paint like
long leaf-veins reaching out, each one a
little mountainous area all to itself, and yet
forming into a star shape, so that the
apartment bedroom's sky looks like it's
splattered with painted celestial suns.

The same ceiling as in my childhood—
I can almost hear the heart-jumping yet sweet barks of
cheer from my runt dog named Casper, and
hear his elongated, rough nails tip-toe across
the hard kitchen floor like my old, charcoal
tap-dance shoes that I used to devotedly wear
in dance class when I was three.
What I wouldn't give if dogs couldn't live
forever—or at least until the owners
themselves parted the Earth.

If I close my eyes, I can almost sense
my mom coming home late from work from yet
another job, and her rushing about to get things
done—start boiling water in the bigger pot
to start dinner, slicing carrots and peeling the
brown potatoes—the ones she let me try to peel,
but I was taking too long before she pulled one out
of my hand to do herself with quick, short slices of the blade.
I was never good at helping with cooking.
And I would be asked to clear the table
more than the boys.

I remember those flea-ridden summer days of
dripping sun flames, sitting dimpled within the old sofa
in the room that the cat was allowed in, settled
with my stained, yellow socks unrolled high so the
vampires couldn't catch the blood that hid in my ankle's veins
and drink me till red mounds appeared on my
pale skin, hiding my scattered beauty-freckles.
I would grip a book tightly between my two hands,
my eyes moving entranced at the new world it was
taking me to, and fantasy characters—people
I desired deeply to meet, but they hid between the lines
of my reverie.

My memories weren't always perfect or pleasant,
but they were dear to my heart as days that I spent
growing—loving and hating my family as people usually do,
yet expanding even more on the memories of love and the
happy times together. In older age, I realized they
would just fade away forever into nothingness, and
the truth of the present—the dreams I wanted to accomplish—
can't resurrect the foolish, schoolgirl hopes of
wanting to have the world, have it all—and
I look at my ceiling now and wish and want nothing more
than for all that love I had, back.

77 It's All Worth It for the Concert

Music.
The coldest January she had known yet.
Seeing her breath, she knows it is below freezing.
At ten o'clock PM shivers in her hipster leggings
to rush into the over-heated building
with her best friend, both excited.

She stands in the swarm of humans,
body against sweating body, shyless—
a nudge, a tap, an odd caress from the strangers.
Fragmentary views of the wooden stage,
clunky speakers and prepared microphones.

Sleek, furry coat now baking her alive,
stashed promptly between her legs for the remaining
five merry hours of jumping and screaming.
Singing along, crisp voice, desiring the stage
for her own auspicious, roaming heart.

Plastic cup in her hands, liquid sloshing—
not powerful enough to tame her, still,
though she tries. Not enough, never enough.
Scorching skin, sweaty drips on forehead—
squeezed and can't leave the crowded room.

Opening bands kiss the mics with their
songs of love and voices of beauty.
With star-splattered eyes they watch, mesmerized
by the allure of it all, feeling whatever the music
feels and trying to capture the moment with cell-video.

The lights taper even more, and the stage
emits its own radiance, flaring and reaching for her,
like she could grab it and wrap it around her like a scarf.
The music of the last band pounds in their ears,
people pushing like pumping out the
good parts of the lemon, ejecting seeds and now coat-buttons.

Vision of the stage—gone. Bulky shadows—
heads of people towering, blinding, unmoving as
statues stuck inside a graveyard ground, but more compacted.
Then a sound is heard, her heart lifts—soars,
guitar string—shrill note of beauty-drums—
throbbing tones of joy! And all at once—
Paramore.

78 Kids Are Kids, Right?

I heard them all spit curses
at me—casting for and
calling upon the day that I would
lay in my chilly grave, surrounded by
short walls of a wooden casket, my
poisoned skin waiting for the dirt
to trickle on the wrinkles in my forehead
blending in my body.
Death wishes—
that is what happens when you try to teach
today's children.

79 Surrounded by Wind

Snapping of the creaking, changing gears.
Me on top—bones pumping together—riding.
The smooth-but-squeaky wheel turns and aches

to go exploring—it gets more curious as it inches
on the car-splattered pavement.
Bikes are beautiful complainers—

wanting to investigate the beckoning woods—
hearing chattering creatures somewhere amongst the trees,
perhaps from invisible tiny heroes or villains—

but the shadows creep darker against the milky moon,
and dangers outnumber.
A young, chocolate-haired girl walks her little black

Chihuahua puppy on a thin leash
and I wonder why her arms hug each other so tightly—
too draining and summer-hot to be shivering.

Cautiously lift one hand and speedily
brush heat-developed sweat back, collected
like unhelpful hair gel.

Press legs faster—*fly*.
Imagining my shoulder blades sprouting painlessly
with white-feathered wings fluffed.

Heart jumps and slides up and down my throat
as I steady myself from an
almost-fall.

Keep going.
Wind
Uphill—pedal hard.

Imagination reels;
I am being tracked—
muscles work and grind—

until my ride is over as
I pull in the narrow space I'd been afraid of—
right between the black steel stair railing and the

friendly cement wall—pathway to my door,
opening unsteadily with my foot as I urge the bike
inside with my other foot and arms,
snug.

80 Ode to My Coffee Drink

O you, who makes my heart joyously
dance, blood-leap, and pound,
my spirit almost faints
fast from my body
at the thought of you.

I await all the slow-clock day
to take a sip of you—
bubbling, frothy, free,
double, toil, espresso—
beloved and all mine,
your smooth flesh flooding
my awaiting throat—opening
to let you encompass my insides.

You are
the one I live forever for and
the one who makes it all
worth it in the hard mornings,
and because of you
I am alive in the very end.

I drink you,
you fill me
sweetly,
and this is
my Heaven.

81 Glaciers Often Fall

Icy whispers of awaited wind whips my hair
up and around the chilled skin on my air-bleached

face, my eyes adrift, gazing at the last of the
icebergs, as the cruise ship leaves Alaskan shores,

and I wonder when I'll see them again.
I witnessed calving ice falling off the mountainous

glaciers, sound altered—
a burst—fracture of itself—

an anxious time-lapse,
as I saw ice drifting away from its partner, of whom

it had been melded to from the beginning—
breaking, cracking, snapping itself off

from the place that it called home,
and falling at a slow pace, as if

it was hesitating its move;
but it was too late, and crashed into the

gray waters of ice and hopelessness.
It floated alone.

The crisp air in my lungs clings onto me tightly
and whispers in my ears a goodbye, wanting

me to remember it, even years later.
The spying,

whitish moon rises higher, until the
bouncing sun pitches new colors and takes over

the sky, until no one notices the ivory orb anymore.
I leave the ship, and all the snow-skinned icebergs,

trouncing, blowing gusts, biting at my hair and a
chance to be remembered.

I take with me everything,
all memories, and hope that I will return.

82 Sunflowers for a Special Day

The open faces of the Sunflowers,
so tiny in the faraway eyes of God,
are transformed by the sunray's beams
like a touch from heavenly fingers.

The glowing bride bends on one knee
and breathes in softly, tickling the
tender yellow petals
in the vast field of angelic fate.

She chooses which blooms are the
most vivacious, the ones to go in the
bouquets, clasped in the palms of the
five smiling bridesmaids.

Sunflowers. The day she met her groom,
he gave her three—and how amiable
and conversational were those
breathing bursts of gold that day.

And as she floated like the ocean's pearl
down the aisle to the music of her heart's future,
the flowers on her breast were
promises of love everlasting.

83 On the Dock

Her stale, disentranced eyes gaze out at the motor
boats which pass by her wooden dock.
People are always going out to fish.
And if that girl joins that boy in the boat,
she knows they won't catch much today.
She wonders if she'll see the smooth fin
of another frolicking dolphin rise.
Short feet up, seeing glasses on, she rests
on the cracked, white rocking chair,
dancing back and forth, back and
forth, following the motion of the wind.

Everything is as hard as it seems,
she thinks. Her eyes remember years of work,
since she first got old enough to get her own retail job
and save for her first crappy car and
creepy apartment full of crawling insects that
came alive in the night when the lights turned off.
To this day, she kills fat cockroaches—
whacking them with a dirty broom,
guts splattered on those bristles,
wondering why the insects don't just go back
to their own planet.

Day after day of loading that heavy truck,
overworked muscles spent, for an older lady
of two-years-until-sixty. Still working to this day.
Counting down until she can retire
and rest the wearied body once and for all
in days that embrace sitting on the wharf
and doing nothing else.

She doesn't know what she hopes for,
except she feels the horizon of the future
is there, and it is better than ever. It must be.
A time when people will appreciate her,
love her for all her hard work,
and her grown kids won't ignore her anymore.

She misses all the yester-times, and constantly
worries about these new days to come and what
horrors, tortures, and mean people it will bring.
And her heart hardens as her body stiffens.
Concentrate on watching the green water slosh
against the wooden pier. A calm breeze that
can soothe passes over her true-thick skin.

The motor boat grunts loudly, cuts the water,
the rising waves rock and knock the dock back
and forth. She sits unmoved, piercing eyes on the small vehicle
that had entangled the teenage boy and girl,
thinking, day-dreaming, wondering about everything.
How will she get through the next day?
Only God knows. And she takes comfort in the fact
that someone else knows instead of her.
Her eyes graze the foamy sea water,
wondering if she'll see a dolphin.
Hoping.

84 Faultless Paintings

Only his paintings were faultless.
Crucifixes were dispersed throughout
the breaking house, diffusing the only
sort of visual comfort.

Hard-knuckle punched windows
left behind glass shards constantly reaching
for the family throughout the day,
and they also left some
hand blood.

Most nights he came home,
sometimes for the entire span of
the stars' slow samba in the sky;
but he never let them sleep.

Every night, his rounded belly is
a gallon of wet red wine,
protruding out as if it
arrogantly held hefty gold instead.

The constant alcohol inked his brain.
Brush strokes of raven-feathered hair moved.
He dipped paint of black, brown, gray.
His model was all purity.

The paints age together, mold together,
blend into the most perfect art of beauty.
His stiffened brush hairs crack.
But the painting doesn't break.

85 Goose-Lady

She held her feathered geese close,
their obnoxious honks sweet in
her ears, like a fresh baby's cry.

The wild lady tapped dry hands over
the keys, plastic fingernails clicking.
She updates status with every day events

of her fat chicken and wild dogs not getting along,
and how she prefers her goose-child
to other peoples' odd

"human children."
She gives it food, comfort, love and
selfies as it squawks for more.

Full animal house, she sees
as she walks around, like in her head;
but the ghost of her lust thrives.

Slightly deranged status update—
a hit—ten comments appear,
but then we realize they're all her own.

86 The Future Has Sharp Turns

She gets up in the early morning,
thinking more about brewing the blackened
good-start coffee than about making
the wrinkled bed with the sleeping
man wrapped tenderly inside.
But she doesn't have to wonder.

Getting through the day is an internal strife;
teaching struggling students who don't give a
damn about doing a single thing in life,
and she wonders how to get through to them
without them wanting to throw books at her.
But she doesn't have to wonder.

She waits for the day that she sees in her mind,
to be the one raising the family, to have
a husband that comes home to kiss her on the lips
and hold her curvy hips like she is worth
so much to him—and she looks at him and smiles—
she doesn't have to wonder. She knows.

87 Most Tender Moment

In the refrigerator-like hospital room
blanched walls were drained of color,
freshly-made mother was pale,
the heart-pounding father even paler, and
the soft-haired toddler boy
closed his oval, stark-cobalt eyes,
and kissed the softest head in the world—
his new baby sister.

88 New Heart

Black high heels echo onward
in the empty hallway like
a skipping record to an eerie soundtrack jumps
as she listens to it alone.

The school is uninhabited by students
as it stands now; just wait a few days,
and they will have to show. No
choice but to be ready.

Hollow classrooms that were darkened,
asleep for those months,
were a hibernation of dusty windows and
spider-web frosted books.

View bright red painted apples on the
desk and within her handmade posters—
she doesn't know what the fruit symbol
stands for anymore. Moldy image.

Opportunity here is a tough gift—
the chance of surviving is an arduous,
pity-twisting obstacle course—
doomed to fall and not be caught.

Strong feet will get mud-splattered,
sore legs will groan with tiredness,
and yet to teach is to be one step
away from God-like.

89　Nightmares at Bay

My senses enhanced in my dream;
colors shook slightly with good vibration,
a sheltered shiver,
like the fast flutter of a hummingbird's rapid
turquoise wing.

I remember the woman from yesterday;
her convulsing body swaying in anger,
agitated heartbeat shouting.
I remember what she did
after.

The mind has memories
that the dreams replay,
but in an alternate world.
It feels better because the dreams
haven't turned into nightmares yet.

90 Graveyard Walk

A walk among the wilting weeds
of once verdant grass sprouting against the
chilled, aged gravestones.

We go together, side by side,
not touching, just
like the corpses.

The wind lifts the sinewy strands
of my hair, whips around
my neck like fingers, tightly.

I smile at him, as we walk by—
the husband who left two children
and a wife behind with his death.

I try not to step on the graves,
but it intrigues me to know
someone cold is beneath me.

We sit on the slouching, wooden
bench, hoping it doesn't over-tip or splinter us.
The smoke breaks through our lips.

The sun glistens against the grave,
shining down on the stone above this buried person
who did not live till today.

Deep beneath the dirt, I wonder
what he looked like, how his dehydrated eyes
would be sucked in his skull.

I don't shiver, but smile
knowing that somewhere his spirit is free
on the Spirit Plane, walking and happy.

On the bench we share a thought,
and my heart flutters when
he reaches to touch my hand.

So alive that skin, the flesh that sweats,
that pumps blood through his heart,
makes me want it for my own.

We sigh and gaze into that sea of stone humps,
and wonder what our lives will be like,
our future, and eventually our death.

We are confident we'll be together
and that is what keeps our hearts safe.
Wrapped together till the end.

91   *Waiting Trails On*

She waits for the phone to ring.
Tries to keep her eyes on the golf channel.
Those hard little balls being hit so far,
traveling such a long way, usually hidden.
Most of them are found again though. It's rare
for them to be just discarded. Left for dead.
Masters of the balls find them.
Almost like they are tamed beasts.

She wrings her hands together,
massaging the place in her hand
where her gold wedding ring—
intricate diamond—once had been.
She took it off when he died.
Didn't wear it since the funeral.
And it's emptier now, but she won't wear
it again.

The tiny little box that can play music,
electrical thing that is molded to
people's hands—bothersome. Infants are born out of
the womb with these devices of awe attached.
Yet hers does nothing for her, in her older age.
She's grown wiser, yet lonely somewhere.
She waits for the phone to ring.
It is her birthday, after all.

He lay on the stark bed,
old arms sunken skinny and no doubt
cold like gray, shivering in the constant
frigid airflow that hospitals spout, as
annoying as blown air-horns to the sick
and sensitive of hearing.

He had been avoiding mirrors
for years, but he could finally say
the mounting wrinkles took over. Time
and the inlaid alcohol had won.
His heart was finally weary and softer,
he could feel it.

He turned over and looked at his
family that he had betrayed,
mistrusted, misfed, abused, and
thought not deeply enough about
these things. Only couldn't wait to taste
the kind of liquor they had in Heaven.

93   In the Distance

The sound reminds me of an
open-mouthed gaping ghost—one
who is scared of its own reflection—
surprised it has one at all.
A long gasp.

It moans like white-foaming waves lift
and pull on itself.
The exercise of the ocean—such
a strong one,
like constant yoga.

The wailing noise complains again,
and I hear the tap taps like hard-footed
dancers in metal shoes—the track
that pulls it along.
and I remember—

the train.

SECTION 6

Remembering My Grandfather

94 With You

The coffin was made ready for you.
Black, I'm sure it was, but I tried
not to look at the details. There were
flowers around and the American flags
raised in memory of you. Your fight and
your war.

I did not want to remember
that moment forever. It existed only
as a dream-memory too vague for life.
I could not feel myself inside my skin.
Some kind of dark fantasy. I waited
to wake.

Before I went to sleep, I would
ignore the unimportant thoughts—that the blood
would not always be flowing through
your body, and that stilled fluid could
create a corpse. And then it did. But it
didn't even look at me standing there.
The unfriendly cadaver would not talk to me.
I wasn't important enough for spoken words.

The coffee was made ready for us
along with other snacks to drink and
eat. If anyone felt hungry. The people
in black gathered, chattered softly. They
did not really eat, for their stomachs
were full of feelings, and that was enough.

You were above ground the last time
I saw you, wrinkled and withering away,
only because age is victorious.
You were breathing, and you smiled to me,
as though you weren't in a heartless
white room with blank walls you
couldn't escape the stare of, and doctors
who didn't know you—didn't know your life,
didn't know your stories that you would
tell, and retell. I should have listened
more intently.

I did not even see them place
dirt upon you. I was too short to see.
But, I know it was done
because that is what happens when shells
are emptied. Dirt always finds a way.
The headstone cold, the flowers reluctantly
set in place. Grandma cried.
I wanted to erase it all,
caress your dead body, pray to you,
plead to you—take me with you.

95   Grandpa Talked of War

As my Grandpa talked,
my child eyes held changing pictures,
nodding as if I understood.

I saw the dry dust gather in my head,
and the heavy rifle gun he carried;
army men staggered all over with them.

Hard hats to hold their heads in,
protect their minds from what they were doing
and who they were trying to kill next.
All were condemned.

As my Grandpa talked,
I felt the frosty fear of known death—
friends that held hands fast
when doomed to die.

Just like the families
torn apart by the soldiers' steady after-shock,
the ultimate rage of confusion and poison in the
alcohol, like they were suicidal rats
trying to kill themselves,
or kill their memories.

Abused in the battles,
damage like shells in the homes—
and now he can't get it out of his mind,
spinning hearts but never settling.

As my Grandpa talked,
I tried to listen, but I wish now it was done more
carefully. In 2004, passing on like it wasn't time,
because I didn't have enough time with him,
his soul breathed without a body once more.

Safe from the rash explosions
and heavy guilt that he survived
when all else drowned in their own blood,
red fields of winning.

96 The Pledge of Allegiance

A diminishing tradition
fading out like a shot star—
it withers in a drawn out death.

No one stands for the flag that
poses like a vacant idol
in the corner of the room
eating dust particles.

Students seated, chatting, cursing
in their language for no reason,
not hearing a word
as I stand for the pledge.

Red like the blood's downfall,
white like hope, and
blue like a sun-rising sky.
Stars like the ghosts of my
grandfather's eyes.

97   Grandpa and Collecting Rocks

Grandpa taught me how to notice
the rocks on the ground whenever we took
our walks. The colors of them were often mundane,
muddy dirt-ridden brown, or weathered, cloudy-cream white,
but the feel of them in your hand was each so unique—
it took my heart some place.

Grandpa traveled the world.
He used to take the rocks that he most liked, and
collect them. Sometimes the rocks would come from
a mountainous part of Switzerland, or a city's street in Japan,
or sometimes he bent down to pick one off the ground
near the rippled water wherever his cruise-ship ported.

Some rocks felt jagged like a Native Indian's stone-arrow,
others smooth like chalk because of years of
strong-lunged wind or of the grating water of rushing streams.
I could collect them from anywhere, hold them in my curious
hand,
and imagine how old this simple creation was. Older than
Grandpa. Even as a child, they were better than toys.

I always gave the Earth something in return for letting
me take its rock, usually a small strand of my hair.
A gift for a gift. My grandpa didn't teach me that,
but I figured it was a nice touch.
Although, looking back from adulthood, I realize it's
hard to give the planet back as much as it gives us.

Grandpa is now gone. I still spot rocks, and sometimes
when they are really beautiful, I will gather them.
I remember him as I travel, and sometimes I will
take a rock or two with me to see the world so it doesn't
just have to stay in one place like in Switzerland or Japan.
I carry them like memories, holding, remembering.

98 Purple Heart

He flocked with the soldiers into the
chalk-like smoky battlefield—one of many,
and he hoisted the obese gun. He had
become muscled, though
he entered years ago as a scrawny man—
they thought he could not do it,
but he buffed up
and showed those just-be-damned
high officers wrong.

Held that life-sucking
rifle and shot
like a man, aiming with both eyes
scared in wide, open circles.
But he separated from his men
at that one significant point,
not wanting to, but ordered to;
he crawled away in inches to shoot at
that green enemy tank.
It saved his life.

And he could not talk to his wife about
it later.
The horror-deaths.
The wrenching guilt of surviving.
Only after years passed.
He was different—like all the men were
after forced battle,
scarred to the soul.

99   Invisible Face of Yours

I didn't see your face set deep in the casket.
But I imagine it must have been cold,
wrinkling in there all alone.
Your jaw tilted to the side because nothing could hold it up,
muscles failed, and your sky-eyes closed because no one could
stand it if they were staring out at them—only
if there was still life behind it, could it be
bearable.

But now, only in my dreams can that happen—seeing
you conscious. Your heaven-colored eyes with a soul inside
that actually look back at me from
tending your vegetable garden like
you would always do on sunny days that were not too
blazing hot with the southern heat.
Gemini. Like me.
I should have looked at your face.

Dad told me not to look.
That I would want to remember you alive,
when your body still held your soul,
or your soul still held your body—
the glue that held all the pieces together
that in time came undone, with stroke after
stroke. The stress of the combat was years ago,
but it never marooned your memories completely.

Maybe your spirit rests soundlessly now.
Your stories will still be told, Grandpa,
as soon as I have children of my own.
If your spirit listens, as I feel it sometimes does
when you're not too busy, then you will
hear me when I say that.
I can feel you in the doorway if I let myself.
I wanted to look at your face.

I know it won't be too long before I too,
swim in the dirt-ground underneath headstones and
statues of frozen Angels, because life is just too
short—although at first it seems long. But child
years of dolls and grace fade fast into the
all consuming black-hole of time.
But one day, everyone will return to the great peace,
as we always do. Then I'll see your eyes again.

SECTION 7

Change

100 Damask Grasps

Gardens of euphoria
grow in my mind with
colors of beauty on the exposed skins
of each flower,
and I hope that
they think they are
pretty enough as they sprout.
I submerge them deep in my heart and
realize that they are but
glimpses
of eventual hope seen for
my future
where love can grow
like a family deserves.
Looking around,
what have we come to?

101　Entombing Mask

I remember running through the pine-scented woods fast,
envisioning I was a creature, winged and aerial—an Angel
to save the day of an innocent human; or even dashing

through the trees like I was being chased by a prowling lion
who hunts, quests, painlessly raids for good meat to chase.
Of course I pretended I was smarter—that I could

outwit anyone—alien or beast, and in my imagination
my animated heart jumped with vigor. I knew
the woods were as alive as the universe glancing

down upon me—smiling that I was so happy.
And I could feel that watchful gaze as if it was my
own mother's. And maybe it is.

Those youthful times of pretending
and playing with the woods like I would a best friend,
have diminished softly. Useless thoughts now spurt

through my mind instead—about work and payments and
how to make the future better for myself.
I've forgotten how to live in the moment, and

what exactly can I do to bring back the childlike desires—
incorporating the gleeful spirit of games into my
everyday life, and sharing a shining joy with everyone I

meet so that it doesn't seem like all adult life is—
is a dark mask that entombs any feeling of happiness?
We aren't alive like this.

102 Safety Net

The spinning life of beauty,
the swirling Earth is the home for our bones
and the stars are the safety net
for our future-escaping souls.
When we die,
that is where we fall—up.

It seems like life is dangerous—
my heart is useless to protect you
and as strong as you are,
muscles are an illusion. You are not safe.
I reach around me and notice
that I can't see the future.

Faith attempts to make me smile
and understand why many answers are hidden
(perhaps for a good reason).
I can only hope the stars,
in all their soul-shining glory,
know what they are doing.

103 Curled In Ice

This reality is beating
alive in only the mind; the eyes search
outward, straining to see something more
than this.

The air is broken by our own
lives: the water flows in the veins of
Earth, the streamlets meeting at the world's heart,
but the sea is not the crisp-sighted ocean it used to be,
now with tainted negativity,
losing beauty with fetid debris.

With each new breath our planet takes,
she wishes to flood it all away.
The rain is painting colors of hope,
downward they spread and bleed,
washing her sullied face again.

But who knows
if this hope can linger or
mature into something worthwhile?
We see every day the
individual human versus the Mother:
we once were one
but now separate entities.

The physical is too sacred—
touched by the hand of God,
it is divine. How can I
feel comfortable being a part of it?

104 Dragonfly Wing Luck

The tear-dropped ice is
melting one-by-one

inside the reviving drink,
looking like swirled

watercolor-painted wings of a
dragonfly, shaped and pink colored,

the thinning ice floating like a lazy-river
ride of ripples.

My spiraled cup is good luck
around my formed fingers;

my lips magic.
My soul mends.

105 Moment Consumed

With clawed hands slightly
raw and tender,
I grasped the fleeing moment—
its untamed heart hustled and
it moved like a
flickering shadow coursing
against drab city walls
in a half-moon's glow—
but I captured it anyway.
I held it down upon my plate.
Its face ground in the porcelain
and then my knife took
off its struggling head.
It soaked red in its own blood and
then,
I ate it.

106 Braiding Colors

Braiding colors—keeping my soul
from falling out—restraining
the wonders of my being so I am
small. When I am like this,
I can live on this Earth as if I'm like
everyone else. I become
the remainders of the Nothing
that was made.

I still feel locked inside my body,
and time doesn't let me go.
Tears, where the emotions hide,
descend when they realize
the corners of the room aren't expanding.
But there are many things
I do not understand.

Perhaps our minds have been too
stone-like for the Angels to penetrate.
We should loosen our guard to the
lighted ones. Their glorious hands can
lift our hearts with gentle courage,
and we can lie upon soothing arms until
invisible sleeps sends away the weak teardrops.

The motion of every ocean's waves
is the memory the soul recalls
as it flickers inside and outside
the physical bodies.
Thoughts roam
from dream
to unconcerned dream.

107 Wistful through Windows

Wine bottles hang upside down
so the corks can absorb more bitter flavor.

An old lady with a rag on her hunched head
gingerly peers into the shop window and wishes.

The bed sprinkled with red petals are only in
the softest dreams—try to breathe in the now.

The policemen drag the protesting sign-man
in Israel away so forcefully, when he is so brave.

We can do nothing now but look in dirty windows,
and wistfully desire something else

to take us by the hands and look in our
bating eyes, and tell us it is all okay.

It will eventually be
alright.

108 Lucidity

Being "thin enough"—
the truth of it
as lucid as
grasping my hand
through the most vibrant,
color-lustful flowers
that are planted deep in my
imagination,
and expecting
my fingers to reveal
a handful of real, petal-strewed blossoms.
But I still want it.

109 The Lost Key in the Sunless Dark

Twisted hearts
can be dragged to the magic
of the healing waters in Lourdes
and changed.

Possibilities are
a mighty allure.

The ringing cedar trees of
Russia—imagine touching the peculiar
bark, rubbing the oil from it,
and becoming ageless.

Belief is the lost
key in the sunless dark.

Can a child of God,
medium of tenacious love,
softly drip restoration out of
His hand's breathing pores?

We are saved by
our acceptance.

The world has a goal—
we connect in some way—
how can we share the fingerprints of
our Creator?

110 Witch Trial Stoning

Your invisible words—
the time I almost saw you cry,
I felt
like in the Salem Witch Trials
when the righteous ones in the buckled
black hats,
Pilgrims of God,
laid the weighted Earth stones
crafted into torture devices,
one by one onto the accused human's chest,
supple, once-desirable breasts
purple-bruised and trampled,
whose life-lusting lips carved
words that could barely whisper
their true-soul innocence,
repeated even as
the fragile ribs began to splinter;
and still the stones pressed down, down
trying to find the beating object
it craved most to crush,
the blood-splattered
angelic
heart.

III   *The Years of Wrinkles*

Years of summer's sun
sucked her beauty away like
my bitter mouth on that poisonous
snake-venom filled cut.

You are healed.

With eyes of envy,
she looks at her daughter
and frowns.

112   *Our Greatness*

A workshop laid with woodened shelves and
tools of silvery iron—

it scattered the thoughts as the
slippery, sweaty-skinned man worked.

Five-o-clock shadow comes
sooner than you think.

The Romans in togas did better than this—
all of present-day contraptions combined.

It's a shy life—of thinking.
A negating lie.

The flattened hammer-face smashes hard
until the iron jumps, sparks golden.

It doesn't lie within me.
When will our greatness be proved?

113 Erupting Words

When buried words
erupt from the grave,
ground quivering and biting dust flying
in your defensive eyes,
remember that words have no
power—
nothing seductive enough;
and they are just
lost dreams
condemned
to wander forever in
deep rooted forests,
without action
to propel them.

114 Unbound

Raw strings of hair, course from the week, avalanche
over the blue polyester couch armrest.

She stretches out wide and yawns over the pained day,
her wrinkled nightshirt a cotton ecstasy.

Braless, she felt she was unbarred;
strangled breasts inhaling airflow once again.

Overworked days too exhausting—
it never stops.

Parched for love, she wanders through the day
with tears of salt building in her veins.

Clothes too tight,
never can buy anything that fits just right.

Lewd red lines cover her body
and grow, frequent as road names on maps,

and her body is a diagram to either
paradise or hell.

Protruding stars one by one come in the sky,
announcing that the time is dark, the moment is night.

She is finally unconfined to the hassles
of the world; her own drowsy skin,

beaten bones, hair, and feet sigh:
unrestrained, unsuppressed.

Her mind ambles in dreams.
Her heart escaped, free.

115   Soul Gallery

Everything real is the present.
The hardened paint of the past

reflects as the omniscient future does,
like an imperfect photographed memory,

illusive and hard to get right.
My life made a picture

of my body's soul
hanging slanted in my mind.

Raise your hand
and bid.

116 *Change My World*

If I think hard enough
and long enough,
reality will flicker and
simmer in the shadows.

I will wait, and
then in the sunlight can
blink a dim, glamour
of the sparks of hope.

I will begin to change,
transforming into truth,
and my world shall
shift with me.

117 Buried Thoughts

The squeak of the turning, silver faucet
and bath water rushes, races, pours
out.
I push the plug snugly
to capture the flood wanting to escape—
tie it up
like holding a wanton waterfall hostage,
telling the streamed-droplets where to make a
splash-landing
or else.
Stepping inside the roasting pool,
succulent steam mists and
laughing bubbles chase and tag
each other until they brush and
stroke my screaming skin and
muscles of stone.
Loosen them.
A bath of peace.
A bath of forgetfulness.
I let the water
reach up and kiss my lips,
cover my nose,
enshroud my eyes.
Buried body,
underwater,
buried thoughts.

Unpainted white walls shine around her; up go
scrapbooked photographs framed like real artwork.

Watching as men shift and grunt, sweat and stumble,
dragging heavy furniture to where she points

like her finger is magical. Even though she can't make decisions
very well, letting drama endure, she can figure it out later.

Siamese cat with the ocean eyes tip-toes around the new
space, rooms all to herself, doors always open. Purrs.

Fresh, afternoon-sun popping through thin blinds,
welcoming them—this new home, the one she prayed for.

She learned to live in the moment. And now, this temporary
home, a repose for her soul. Prayers do let dreams come alive.

119 *The Last Doll*

When she was born
they said, "Let us put her
into a box." Everyone agreed
with smiling, nodding heads;
so into a box she went.

Lathered with toys and rattles
and a blanket that weathered
it through, she was comfy and
safe. They realized that the rain
soon became a problem. It would
drip about her eyes and ears.

So, the lid went on next with
new, shiny, golden nails
to cover her perfect head.
The baby reached up and
realized that this was her new
sky.

They realized this child was
never going to be safe enough
from the world. "Let us place
her underground," they said, "so
they can't see her." Never would
anyone touch her.

So they gave her the last doll
that she would ever embrace
and dug a hole to fit the box
snugly. Tucking her in with
a last kiss goodnight,
she slept underground.

120 Spirit of Feathers

Some of the fragmented bones
are still beating with life inside,
but then surrender,
awaiting quickened death
within the broken body
as the spirit of the bird
leaves like a drifting mist—
a gust of feathers.

121 Winter Destination

The trees of my past loom overhead
and come cover me with their shadowy leaves.
They comfort me with their longing gaze
but I shiver in the changing season.

The Autumn then dies and becomes Winter,
and again will be born my wish for a scenic,
sugar-coated bedding of snow.
As I am lost walking among the fragile flakes,

the things I have forgotten and all the things
I am will fade away as my steps grow heavy;
I trudge along until my lead-like feet move easier,
things feel like they rise more than fall,
and I feel like I am my destination.

122 Mirrors and Reflections

Beautiful glass.
Lights gleam around the edges
like a rapturous star.

But then,
my reflection smirks—
the dense and dark surprise
of my amassed imperfections.

My eyes can't erase
the loathing,
the flawed image embalmed in me:
irreversible.

Reiki out my soul
with my scratching fingers;
I fall out of my body.
Separated—I see.

I gain perspective
among the clouds. Isolated from it—
my body is nothing.
A creation that can be admirable.

God makes a wish—throws
a coin in the fountain—glimmers.
My anointed soul
seeps back into my body.

123 Lost Soul

I am lost
among the twisted trees,
sensing the hot-winded breath
that flows through the changed leaves.
I could be in the sticking shadow
that grins near his shoulder,
or the ripples in the waves
playing in his red heart.

I am lost
somewhere deep with a feeling
that has not matured yet.
I could be in the depth of his mind
or in the smooth rock kicked,
beaten down by time and fate.
I could be no where at all.
But I hope someone thinks
and finds me.

124　The Power Within

Disappointment can be overcome,
a shining star warming the numb—
intriguing the soul,
stimulating the mind's rapid words
of hope and desperate peace
within the self's abyss,
and without into the universe;

all spaces are God,
for into the future,
where nonexistent time is silent,
nothing can keep still
the million signs of change
as we alter and stir the silvery
lining of the horizon and see
a new beginning for us again.

125 Skeleton Sighs

My chest hollows.
My heartbeats slow and then
mold with time.
My eyes suck inside
until they are all rotting brain.
My toes tremble and
turn to bony ashes
like all else in my
body.
Physicality decays as
I wait for
this that they say—
this sanity—
this Peace on Earth.
I form a slow skeleton.

126 Fruitful Thoughts

She cuts the fruit one by
one with the serrated knife,
and pays no attention to the frequent purple
juice that squirts out of the seeded cherries
and blueberries that are going squishy.

She slices them as they bleed out onto the
staining wooden cutting board, and drops each
piece of fruit into the empty wine glass
as she ponders over the sensational
three-dimensional object,

and wonders
many things, like how to make the glass
transform into a different entity, or how to blend
into the wall and make herself invisible.
She pours the blood-wine and drinks.

127 Blending Colors

Capture
my drip-painted heart

with Nature's sprawling,
branched hands,

and turn my eager ear
to the sweet whisper rapture

until my limbs go
still from leaning in

to listen for the assured voice
of the lush, breeze-like flow

of spirit.
I am all I ever dreamed of,

a freckle in the
universe,

a part of you,
and I blend.

128 Gate of the Stars

Almost invisible, the thin
gate to the stars creaks
open—

airless space creeps
in my dying lungs and
feels welcome in

my thick blood;
makes itself at home
in my dense body.

Floating, I feel lighter here,
like my heart is wind
instead of worry.

The fire-burnished stars and
planets circle like an endless
festival of dreams.

The universe has lusted
after me since I was a
child—

and I am here to be desired,
touched, and changed
by the heavens forever.

129 Optimism Rests in Stars

An optimistic heaven above
shines and mocks me
as I look up to see whether it's a moving plane
or a florid star,
and then I hear the roar.

I don't believe in what they say—
that the stars are so far ahead of us in time
that they are dead when we see their light—because
that takes out the possibility that I could one day
live on one, and I'm pretty optimistic.

About the Author

Celestial K. was an instant poet in her younger years. She grew up in Augusta, Georgia and has involved herself in creative activities such as: writing, theater, singing, working with children, and yoga. She graduated from Wesleyan College with a BA in English and a minor in Music, and then from Augusta State University with a MA in Teaching.

She is a success. Several of Celestial K.'s poems are published in the online magazines Eye On Life, Current Accounts, and Congruent Spaces. Interestingly, Catherine Doyle Sullivan, who designed the gorgeous cover art for *Soul Thoughts*, is also her Aunt.

Celestial K. is currently a Language Arts teacher and claims there is never a dull moment. Personally she strives to develop spiritually and grow in love, and she insists the world do the same.

In her words, Celestial K. says: "I hope to share my words so that you feel something beautiful and fulfilling when you finish reading. I also want to move you to be inspired—let your own creativity and passion guide your soul so that you are satisfied in every area of your life. You can do all you desire. This is what I'm learning."

In the future, Celestial K. will continue to follow her passion with writing and publishing poetry as well as novels, and she looks forward to people reading her work.